scjc

HORSEPOWER

SPORTS CARS

by Matt Doeden

Reading Consultant:
Barbara J. Fox
Reading Specialist
North Carolina State University

Capstone press

Mankato, Minnesota

Blazers is published by Capstone Press
151 Good Counsel Drive, P.O. Box 669, Mankato, Minnesota 56002
www.capstonepress.com

Library of Congress Cataloging-in-Publication Data
Doeden, Matt.
    Sports cars / by Matt Doeden.
    p. cm.—(Blazers horsepower)
    Includes bibliographical references and index.
    ISBN 0-7368-2734-X (hardcover)
    1. Sports cars—Juvenile literature. I. Title. II. Series.
TL236.D64 2005
629.222'1—dc22   2004003795

Summary: Discusses features of famous models of sports cars,
    including the Viper, Corvette, Porsche, Ferrari, and Lamborghini.

Editorial Credits
Tom Adamson, editor; Jason Knudson, designer; Jo Miller, photo
    researcher; Eric Kudalis, product planning editor

Photo Credits
Drew Phillips, 5, 6–7, 9, 11, 27
Getty Images Inc./Bill Pugliano, 24
Mercury Press/Isaac Hernandez, cover, 19
Ron Kimball Stock/Ron Kimball, 13, 15, 16–17, 20, 21, 23, 26, 28–29

1 2 3 4 5 6 09 08 07 06 05 04

TABLE OF CONTENTS

CORVETTE TEST

A driver pulls a red Chevrolet Corvette Z06 onto a test track. He stomps on the gas pedal. The tires squeal.

Within seconds, the car is going 100 miles (160 kilometers) per hour. The driver speeds up. He is testing the engine's power.

The driver cranks the wheel on a sharp curve. The car moves smoothly. The driver speeds up again.

BLAZER FACT

Corvettes are made in Bowling Green, Kentucky.

Sports Car Design

Sports cars are fast. They are low to the ground. Sports cars are built for looks and speed.

Most sports cars have 8-cylinder engines. Some engines have up to 12 cylinders. More cylinders mean more power.

BLAZER FACT

Sports car engines have cylinders in the shape of a V. This one is a V-10 engine.

Some sports cars have a spoiler. The spoiler looks like a wing. It helps the driver control the car.

Spoiler

PORSCHE 911
TURBO COUPE DIAGRAM

Spoiler

Hood

Tire

U.S. SPORTS CARS

Dodge built the first Viper in 1989 as a test car. The Viper has the most powerful engine built in the United States.

2004 Dodge Viper SRT-10

Top speed: 190 miles per hour
(306 kilometers per hour)
0–60 mph: 3.9 seconds
Cost: $80,000

In 1953, Chevrolet built 300
Corvettes. Today, Corvettes are
smaller and faster. They are lower
to the ground.

BLAZER FACT

The first Corvettes were white with red interiors.

2004 Chevrolet Corvette Z06

Top speed:	171 miles per hour (275 kilometers per hour)
0–60 mph:	3.9 seconds
Cost:	$52,000

EUROPEAN MODELS

The Porsche 911 has been one of the world's most popular sports cars since 1964. The Porsche 911 Cabriolet is a convertible.

2004 Porsche 911 Turbo Cabriolet

Top speed:	189 miles per hour (304 kilometers per hour)
0–60 mph:	4.3 seconds
Cost:	$128,200

In 1929, Enzo Ferrari started his car company in Italy. The Ferrari Scaglietti is the newest model. The first Scaglietti was built in 2004.

2004 Ferrari 612 Scaglietti

Top speed: 196 miles per hour
(315 kilometers per hour)
0–60 mph: 4.2 seconds
Cost: $240,000

The Lamborghini Murcielago is very powerful. It has a 12-cylinder engine. The car's low build is perfect for sharp corners.

BLAZER FACT

Murcielago was the name of a famous and tough bull that fought in bullfights.

2004 Lamborghini Murcielago

Top speed:	205 miles per hour (330 kilometers per hour)
0–60 mph:	3.8 seconds
Cost:	$384,600

1999 FERRARI 360 MODENA

GLOSSARY

convertible (kuhn-VUR-tuh-buhl)—a car with a top that can be put down

cylinder (SIL-uhn-dur)—a hollow chamber inside an engine in which fuel burns to create power

mph—the abbreviation for miles per hour

spoiler (SPOIL-uhr)—a wing-shaped part attached to the rear of a sports car that helps improve the car's handling

READ MORE

Graham, Ian. *Sports Cars.* Designed for Success. Chicago: Heinemann, 2003.

Kimber, David. *Auto-mania!* Vehicle-mania! Milwaukee: Gareth Stevens, 2004.

McKenna, A. T. *Lamborghini.* Ultimate Cars. Edina, Minn.: Abdo, 2002.

INTERNET SITES

FactHound offers a safe, fun way to find Internet sites related to this book. All of the sites on FactHound have been researched by our staff.

Here's how:

1. Visit *www.facthound.com*
2. Type in this special code **073682734X** for age-appropriate sites. Or enter a search word related to this book for a more general search.
3. Click on the **Fetch It** button.

FactHound will fetch the best sites for you!

INDEX